30 DAYS OF DEPTH WITH JESUS

30 Days of Depth with Jesus

NICCORI THOMAS-BROWN

Kaelyn Jackson, the Artist

Superior Publishing LLC.

Copyright © 2021;2022 Niccori Thomas-Brown

Illustrated by Kaelyn Jackson

All rights reserved. No part of this publication may be reproduced, distributed, or transmitted in any form or by any means, including photocopying, recording, or other electronic or mechanical methods, without the prior written permission of the publisher, except in the case of brief quotations embodied in critical reviews and certain other noncommercial uses permitted by copyright law.

ISBN: 978-1-9533056-10-8

Superior Publishing LLC
Cedar Bluff, Mississippi

Dedication

I dedicate this book to the best teacher I know –the Holy Spirit. Thank you for Your guidance, direction, and feedback.

In the beginning was the Word, and the Word was with God, and the Word was God. He was in the beginning with God.
John 1:1-2 NKJV

Knowing Jesus Christ means to have a relationship with Him. Relationships are strengthened by spending time together. How can a person spend time with Jesus? You can spend time with Jesus by reading and meditating on His Word.

According to John 1, the Lord and His Word are one in the same. When you devote time to learning and understanding God's Word, then you are deepening your relationship. Use this devotion to go deeper in your relationship with Jesus by meditating on His Word, coloring while you reflect, think, and reconnect to the one true living God.

It Comes With Maturity

Day 1
Prayer: Gracious Heavenly Father, please help me to stay in your will. Help me to always be obedient to your voice. Renew my mind to the things of Your Kingdom.

Word of God: Romans 12:2 NKJV And do not be conformed to this world, but be transformed by the renewing of your mind, that you may prove what is that good and acceptable and perfect will of God.

I am going to be honest and admit that when I am tired, I am guilty of cutting some corners or just not doing what I am supposed to do. There have been times when I have had an extensive list of things to do at work and a directive from the Superintendent's desk trickles down to the teachers. Just when I thought I could not possibly have anything else on my plate, one more item is added. In addition to this, it is due the very next day!

So, what should you do? Should you pretend you

did not get the memo or email? Should you go and complain to others? Should you send a lengthy email expressing your disapproval of how things are done to your manager, supervisor, principal, or superintendent? It is sad and embarrassing to say that I am guilty of doing all the above.

As you mature in Christ, your mindset will change. Maturity in Christ brings about a different way to respond when an issue arises. We are in control of how we respond and what we say. We should respect authority as well, which is honored by God. Carnality begins to peel away from our mind as we grow. Our minds become renewed. We can renew our minds with the Word of God. We should decree and declare, daily, that we have a mind like Christ.

Before you blow a gasket about the never-ending to-do list, breathe, and ask God to increase your hunger for His Word. The Word of God is a weapon to fight off negative thoughts. Your mind will be renewed when you meditate on His Word. I thank God for His unchanging, powerful, promising Word.

It Would Not Hurt

Day 2 Prayer: Heavenly Father, thank you for giving me life. Let your light shine through me by spreading your joy in other people's lives. In Jesus' name I pray, amen.

Word of God: Proverbs 16: 22 NKJV Pleasant words are like a honeycomb, Sweetness to the soul and health to the bones.

How many of us have seen a fellow coworker or family member with a glum look on his or her face? I have. I have also been that person. One problem was that I would be exhausted and frustrated by the lack of resources available to do my job effectively. There were days when it seemed as if I was just going through the motions and watching the clock. Do not get me wrong. I love teaching, but for various reasons I was burnt out. I noticed the same worn out looks on my coworkers faces as well. How were we going to make it another day, week, or month?

I came to the realization that I could not change

everything that I felt was wrong with my work environment in my own strength. Nor could I change anything in a day. So, I decided to stop throwing a pity party and tell the devil that he could not have my joy. Our joy comes from the Lord. The Lord is our strength. With the strength given to me through the Holy Spirit, I started to spread joy at work. I thought to myself that it would not hurt anyone but uplift them. It could only help. It did not require a lot of time either. I would write inspirational quotes and scriptures on index cards and leave them on teachers' desks before school started or slip it into their mailboxes on my way to the cafeteria. I began to see a shift in my work environment. We were smiling more. We were more energetic. We were having fun teaching again. Students were having fun learning again. All it took was a fifty-cent pack of index cards and the Word of God.

You Would Be Surprised

Day 3

Prayer: Heavenly Father, I am grateful for Your presence. I pray that I always find comfort, peace, and reassurance in You. In Jesus' name I pray, amen.

Word of God: Exodus 33:14 NKJV And He said, "My Presence will go with you, and I will give you rest."

It seems as if we are constantly rushing to one place or another. I find myself rushing just about every part of the day. During the morning rush, I am making sure my children eat breakfast, my car is packed for work, and seeing my oldest daughter get on the school bus. Then I rush off to work to beat the clock. I rush to my classroom to ensure everything is set and ready for the day. Sometimes I find myself rushing from one subject to another to follow the schedule posted outside my door.

I find myself rushing after school to get to my dismissal post. Once all the students are gone home, I hurry home to prepare dinner, help my children with homework, and do the usual evening routines. How many of you find yourself rushing daily? Surely, I am not the only one.

When we take time to rest, it helps us physically and mentally. The Lord wants us to find rest in Him. God even rested, in Genesis chapter one, after creating for six consecutive days. When we rest in our Lord and Savior, He comforts us with indescribable peace and love. I encourage you to spend the first time of your day with Christ.

You would be surprised to discover that despite how busy we think we are, when we pray, worship, and rest in Christ during the first part of our day, it sets the tone for the remainder of that day. In conclusion, let us give God our time.

PERCEPTION

Day 4 Prayer: Heavenly Father, you are an all knowing and all-seeing God. I am grateful for the plan You have for my life. Help me to always speak positively over every situation that arises. Father, bring your Word to my remembrance so I may speak life. In Jesus's name I pray, amen.

Word of God: Proverbs 18:21 KJV Death and life are in the power of the tongue: and they that love it shall eat the fruit thereof.

I remember when I was a student-teacher during my final semester of undergraduate studies. During that last week of school, the teachers were doing final checklists, updating cumulative folders, and creating a class roster for the upcoming school year. I listened as they grouped the students and assigned them to certain teachers.

It is vital that we speak life. The words that we use should build others up instead of causing harm. As a teacher, I have put certain labels on students and passed the word to the next teacher about this label.

At that time, it seemed right or as if I was just helping a fellow teacher by "warning" him or her. On the contrary, I was speaking death over that student. I am not talking about physical death, but negativity. If we label others with descriptors such as bad; does not listen; will not ever get it; a headache; or a pest, then we are not speaking life over them.

Instead, let us encourage our family and neighbors by highlighting their strengths. Each day let us find a positive comment to make about even the most difficult person. All it takes is a change of perception. How do you see them? Let's ask God to help us see them as He sees them. How wonderful would it be to look at them with God's perception!

DECISIONS, DECISIONS

Day 5 Prayer: Dear merciful Father thank you for having mercy upon me. Help me to make wise decisions. I pray that I do things to please you. Lead me Lord. Do not let me go down the wrong path. In Jesus's name I pray, amen.

Word of God: Genesis 3:12 NKJV Then the man said, "The woman whom You gave to be with me, she gave me of the tree, and I ate."

What does it mean to be responsible for our actions? As teachers, we are leaders and role models, who must be mindful of our actions. Our students are always watching and more importantly God is always watching as well. My pastor is always telling us that life is about choices and decisions. Every decision we make reflects on our character. It should be a priority to want to please God.

We cannot turn back the hands of time; therefore, we should be prudent in our decision-making process.

God wants us to think before we act. Throughout the book of Proverbs, those who make rash decisions without thinking are described as simple or foolish. We are made in the image of God who gives us wisdom. The book of Proverbs offers an extensive explanation of how using wisdom saves us from a lot of trouble.

As parents and/or teachers we help young people gain more knowledge and wisdom daily. Let's help them to think and make wise decisions. It is important that they know that there are consequences, good or bad, to every decision. We want them to be prudent. Learning how to think and reflect while they are young, paves the way for them to be wise citizens later in life.

It is not a coincidence that of all the things Solomon could have asked God for he asked for wisdom. Solomon understood wisdom is worth far more than money, because he had wisdom, he

- knew how to acquire great wealth. In conclusion, use teachable moments to mold young people

into prudent thinkers.

Making the Most of It

Day 6

Prayer: Lord, I pray that my faith in you is always strong and never failing. Help me to see the bigger picture and not be distracted with smaller things. I am grateful that nothing is impossible for you. In Jesus's name I pray, amen.

Word of God: John 6:11 NKJV And Jesus took the loaves, and when He had given thanks, He distributed them to the disciples, and the disciples to those sitting down; and likewise of the fish, as much as they wanted.

We have all been faced with challenges in our personal lives and careers. How we respond during these challenges is important. When it looks like you are stuck between a rock and a hard place, you should climb upon that rock and stand firmly. Jesus is our rock. Our faith should be built on Jesus, who is strong and solid. Trials, tests, and challenges make us stronger if we do not give up. That is why Proverbs

24:10 NKJV states, "If you faint in the day of adversity, your strength is small." The Word of God also declares in Proverbs 3:5-6 NKJV "Trust in the LORD with all your heart, and lean not on your own understanding; in all your ways acknowledge him, and He shall direct your paths." God is with us when we are faced with trouble. He is our deliverer. We can experience His awesome power if we just do not fold under pressure.

Jesus and the disciples were faced with the challenge of feeding over five thousand people with only five loaves of bread and two fish. Jesus did not fret or lose His composure. He simply made the most of the situation. He prayed a blessing over the food (John 6:11) and distributed it to the disciples who in turn gave it to the people. Another miracle happened! Jesus is Jehovah Jireh, our provider. He provided more than enough food for the people. There were even leftovers!

In conclusion it's our job to keep the faith and not budge but stand firm on the Word of God. It is then that we will see His hand at work in our situation. Be strong in the Lord my fellow believers!

It Is Only A Test!

Day 7

Prayer: Heavenly Father I trust You. I know that You would not leave me. I thank You for hearing my prayers and answering. I lean into You for strength. In Jesus's name I pray, amen.

Word of God: Matthew 10: 22 NKJV And you will be hated by all for My name's sake. But he who endures to the end will be saved.

If we are going to serve Christ wholeheartedly and in spirit and truth, then we are going to face persecution and tests. Jesus said in Matthew 10:22 that we would be hated by all for His name's sake. Jesus was hated by many. Through persecution we must walk in love. Jesus gave the perfect example of how to walk in love.

Many years ago, a parent of one of my students decided she did not like me and tried her best to cause trouble for me. It went as far as the superintendent coming to visit my classroom. At the time, I did not know what I know now. I became terribly angry and irritated. Thank God, the superintendent found no fault in me and the issue dissolved. I encourage you to respond differently than I did. I encourage you to pray and ask God for discernment. Using discernment is wisdom to know when God is testing you, the enemy is attacking you, and it brings awareness to who is for or against you. Using discernment will save you a lot of trouble. Remember Luke 6:28 KJV "Bless those who curse you and pray for them which despitefully use you."

In closing, I urge you to declare daily that you will walk in love as Christ did. Let us imitate Christ in every area of our lives. Do not lose footing in your faith when persecution comes. Jehovah-Nissi fights for us. Be blessed.

What Are You Wearing?

Day 8

Prayer: My gracious, loving Lord, thank You for being who You are. Thank You for protection. Thank You for equipping me with everything that I need. In Jesus's name, amen.

Word of God: Ephesians 6:11 NKJV Put on the whole armor of God, that you may be able to stand against the wiles of the devil.

So, you're going over your mental checklist before sprinting out the door for work. It may go something like this:

- keys-check
- lunchbag-check
- coffee-check
- bag/purse-check

Something is missing. Are you completely dressed? Did you remember to put on the whole armor of God? There is a reason that God provides us with this armor. We are in a spiritual battle, which is mentioned in Ephesians 6:12. His armor offers protection, as well as a weapon to fight with. That weapon is the sword of the Spirit, which is the Word of God described in Ephesians 6:17. Swords are made to fight, to sever, and to kill. After David used his sling shot to defeat Goliath, he used Goliath's own sword to remove his head (1 Samuel 17:51).

Every part of the armor is vital, but the sword of the Spirit is particularly important. Without our sword, we can only block what the enemy is throwing at us as described in Ephesians 6:16. God has given us His Word or sword of the Spirit to cut down our spiritual attackers mentioned in Ephesians 6:12.

Jesus set an example when He used His sword of the Spirit after His 40 day fast ended. Satan tried to entice Jesus, but each time Jesus boldly and firmly stated "It is written". Jesus defeated the enemy with the Word of God.

The devil cannot stand against the Word. John 1:1 NKJV explains why. "In the beginning was the Word, and the Word was with God, and the Word was God." This scripture clearly lays it out plainly! God is the sword of the Spirit! Therefore, Jesus was cutting the devil down with the Father Almighty! In conclusion, be sure you are fully dressed every day. Be blessed.

The Real Lion

Day 9 Prayer: Lord, You are Supreme. You are the Almighty, one, true, and living God. There is no one greater. You are the one I worship. You are the one I exalt. You are awesome and great. I love you. I will forever sing your praises. In Jesus's name I pray, amen.

Scripture: 1 Peter 5:8 NKJV Be sober, be vigilant; because your adversary the devil walks about like a roaring lion, seeking whom he may devour.

As teachers, we give directions all the time. We expect our students to follow these directions. God has given us an entire instruction manual, the Holy Bible, His Word. Let's look at two directives given in 1 Peter 5:8. First, we're told to be sober. Secondly, we are told to be vigilant.

This means we should have a sound mind, be alert and watchful. The enemy does not take any time off from stealing, killing, and destroying (John 10:10). If allowed, the enemy will bombard your mind will negative thoughts. In your mind is where he starts fighting you first. He wants to steal your joy at home, your peace at work, and destroy opportunities for you and your students. But do not fret. The real lion of Judah, Jesus Christ, intercedes and lives within us, therefore we do not walk in defeat. We walk in victory.

When we are sober, vigilant, have faith, and are fully suited in the armor of God, we will have victory through Jesus Christ. Victory at work! Victory at home! Victory in your students'

The Perfect Teacher

Day 10
Prayer: Lord, You are so amazing. Thank You for guiding me. You always know what is best for I cannot make it without You. Help me to stay focused on You and practice your Word. In Jesus' name I pray, amen.

Scripture: Matthew 7:28-29 NKJV And so it was, when Jesus had ended these sayings, that the people were astonished at His teaching, for He taught them as one having authority, and not as the scribes.

Are things in your classroom or home not going as smoothly as you'd like? That probably has been the case in many classrooms or homes. It may have occurred on more than one occasion as well. I remember the morning the superintendent's office staff was scheduled to visit the classrooms at my former school. Well, the principal had already had the 'talk' with us.

We were all expected to be giving intense vocabulary instruction when the anticipated visitors peeked into our classrooms. I was prepared. My lesson was ready on my Smart Board, students were seated, and then the worst happened.

Just as the superintendent was opening my door, two of my students began fighting. From the observers' point of view, it probably seemed as if I was giving my students idle time instead of teaching. Honestly, that was not the case. That particular school year had been my hardest, but I kept pushing. There was something that I was not using in my classroom that morning. Jesus used it (Matthew 7:29). What did He use that I was not? Authority! I was not using my God given authority described in Luke 10:19.

In conclusion, I encourage you to use your authority in your classroom and home to bind (Matthew 18:18) every spirit of distraction, division, discouragement, and defeat. It is so reassuring to know that the Word of God offers solutions to every problem.

Multiple Hats

Day 11

Prayer: Lord, You are everything to me. Thank you for giving me strength and peace. Help me to continue to love others and let your light shine through me. In Jesus' name I pray, amen.

Word of God: Isaiah 9:6 NKJV For unto us a Child is born, Unto us a Son is given; And the government will be upon His shoulder. And His name will be called Wonderful, Counselor, Mighty God, Everlasting Father, Prince of Peace.

We wear multiple hats. Teaching is just one of my hats. If I see someone having a difficult time with friends or at home, I put on a counselor hat. If a student scrapes a knee at recess, I put on a nurse hat. If I am helping to resolve a conflict, I put on a mediator hat. Jesus also wears many hats. He is a healer, deliverer, redeemer, counselor, provider, among an endless list of awesome characteristics. With that being said, Jesus knows what it is like to multitask. There is not anything about us that He does not understand. Jesus even took a nap when He was tired. "And suddenly a great tempest arose on the sea, so that the boat was covered with the waves. But He was asleep." (Matthew 8:24 NKJV)

It is encouraging to know that our Savior set a beautiful example of multitasking. Let's keep pushing forward and doing what we do best. God gives us strength. "The LORD is my strength and my shield; My heart trusted in Him, and I am helped; Therefore, my heart greatly rejoices, And with my song I will praise Him." (Psalms 28:7 NKJV)

Praying for Children

Day 12

Prayer: Heavenly Father, thank you for all children connected to me. I lift them up to You. I apply Your powerful blood over their lives. I pray that they always seek You for direction. Please give them strong discernment. I bind the enemy's plan for their lives. I decree and declare that they walk in the destiny You have designed for them. In Jesus's name I pray. Amen.

Scripture: 1 Peter 4:8 NKJV And above all things have fervent love for one another, for "love will cover a multitude of sins."

It is important that we pray for the well-being, physical and mental health, home lives, and progress in academics of the children we are connected to. We want them to excel in every part of their lives. If they are not saved, pray for their salvation. We love all of them, but one genuine way to show we love them is to pray for them.

Prayer should not be taken lightly. Prayer is vital. Ephesians 6:18 and 1 Thessalonians 5:17 instruct us to always pray. Daniel prayed three times a day (Daniel 6:10). Jesus modeled to the disciples how to pray (Luke 11:1-4). Throughout the Holy Bible we see numerous people praying. One of my favorite examples of how prayer and fasting works is found in 2 Chronicles 20. In this chapter of Chronicles, Jehoshaphat is up against three armies, Ammon, Moab, and Mount Seir. These armies formed a great multitude, but when God is with you it doesn't matter how many of your enemies' band together. Jehoshaphat instructed all of Judah to fast and pray. They worshipped, praised, and prayed days before the battle. On the day of the battle, they did not even have to fight because God fought for them. They stood before their enemies and sang praises to God while the Ammonites, Moabites, and Mount Seir slaughtered themselves.

Unfortunately, some churches overlook prayer service. Prayer is necessary for a church to effectively fight the enemy, which was demonstrated in 2 Chronicles 20. Prayer makes us stronger. Prayer deepens our relationship with God. Prayer is an intimate time to communicate with God. We will not have success with our students without prayer and the Word. Joshua 1:8 and Psalms 1:1-3 explain the importance and benefits of studying scripture. These set of texts describe the good success and prosperity a person has when they learn and apply the Word of God.

In closing, I urge you to pray and fast on behalf of

children you are called to cover. It will make a tremendous difference in their lives and yours. If you are not accustomed to fasting, then ask God for grace and wisdom. He will fill your heart with so much love and desire to pray for them that you will push through. Prayer works and changes things. Be blessed.

Sweet Baby Jesus

Day 13 Prayer: Lord of my life, King of kings, gracious Heavenly Father, I give you glory and honor on this day. Despite how things around me may look, I will praise You. I thank You for strength to keep making strides forward. I pray that you continuously lead me in the right direction. I am grateful that You go before me and have a plan for my life. I don't ever want to move without You. I surrender every aspect of my life to You. I offer my heart to You. Father, mold me. Shape me. Purge me of anything that's not like You. Help me to love what You love and hate what you hate. Renew my mind. In Jesus's name I pray, amen.

Scripture: Revelation 1:16 NKJV He had in His right hand seven stars, out of His mouth went a sharp two-edged sword, and His countenance was like the sun shining in its strength.

Some of us only like to think of Jesus as the sweet, smiling, nice Jesus. Some of us like to only think of Him as the loving Jesus who hugged the children and let them sit at his feet while He taught. Or we like to think of Him as the gracious Lord who blessed and multiplied the five loaves of bread and two fish to feed thousands of people (Matthew 14: 18-21; Luke 9:16-17;

John 6:11; Mark 6:41). We even like to only look at the miracles of healing He did such as causing the lame to walk and the blind to see (Matthew 15:30; Matthew 21:14). Do not get me wrong. These are wonderful characteristics of our Savior and I love Him dearly.

But when you've been going through hardship; praying and crying; having more month than money; your children sick; family members dying every couple of months; (I am speaking from experience!) chaos at work; people trying to take my teaching license; trying to stop me from graduating; your character being assassinated; people lying on you; faced with losing your

home; and all this happened while serving God.... What do you do? The enemy is whispering lies through all this and asking 'Where is your God?' With all this going on I needed a Jesus who FIGHTS! You see, sometimes we forget about this Jesus! This is the Jesus who saw the foolishness going on in the temple, flipped the tables over in anger, and declared with authority that His house is a house of prayer (Matthew 21:12-13). He is the Lord that I say rises up and fights for me. He will fight on your behalf as well.

Sometimes we forget that He is our vindicator

(Psalms 54:1; 35:24; 26:1). He is the righteous judge (Psalms 7:11). He is Jehovah-nissi (Exodus 17:15). He threw hailstones from heaven to help Joshua win a battle (Joshua 10:11). He is the God who trained David for war (Psalms 144:1). He's the God who had a donkey die in the exact spot Samson stood and slew 1,000 men with its jawbone (Judges 15:14-16)! Samson didn't do that in his own strength. The Word clearly states in verse 14 that the 'Spirit of the Lord came mightily upon him'.

The Word of God is not a menu at a restaurant. We do not just choose what we want to focus on. He has instructed us to meditate on His Word day and night (Joshua 1:8; Psalms 1:2; Deuteronomy 28:1). He did not say meditate only on the amazing miracles. We are to study the Word in its entirety because we are in a battle. Jesus was not just going from town to town with a huge smile plastered on His face and doing miracles. Jesus has always been a bold warrior, who is always victorious!

Do Not Bend

Day 14

Prayer: Heavenly Father, I need you now more than ever. You are the Lion of Judah. You're Almighty and all knowing. Help me to be bold. Help me to be courageous. Strengthen me Lord. Please don't allow me to waver in my faith when I'm faced with pleasing man or standing firm on Your Word. Let me be rooted firmly in righteousness, integrity and love. In Jesus's name I pray, amen.

Scripture: "Look!" he answered, "I see four men loose, walking in the midst of the fire; and they are not hurt, and the form of the fourth is like the Son of God." Daniel 3:25 NKJV

The Word of God clearly tells us how He perceives the world. James 4:4 NKJV explains it well. "Adulterers and adulteresses! Do you not know that friendship with the world is enmity with God? Whoever therefore wants to be a friend of the world makes himself an enemy of God." We cannot be friends of the world. If we do, God will see us as an enemy. I do not want God to see me as an enemy. We should always want Him to call us His friend. "And the

Scripture was fulfilled which says, "Abraham believed God, and it was accounted to him for righteousness." And he was called the friend of God." (James 2:23 NKJV)

So how can we be God's friends? Believe in Him. Serve Him and no other. Have faith in him, which pleases Him. "But without faith it is impossible to please Him, for he who comes to God must believe that He is, and that He is a Rewarder of those who diligently seek Him." (Hebrews 11:6 NKJV) We also must stand firm on His Word, which means no compromising.

His Word has not changed. He means what He says. There is a list of abominations in Proverbs. "These six things the Lord hates, Yes, seven are an abomination to Him: A proud look, A lying tongue, Hands that shed innocent blood, A heart that devises wicked plans, Feet that are swift in running to evil, A false witness who speaks lies, And one who sows discord among brethren." (Proverbs 6:16-19 NKJV)

This is not a comprehensive list, but it's a good place to start. God has standards and He is not lowering them. As Christians, God is upholding us to His standards. Daniel's three friends didn't bend. They stood on their faith even when the heat was turned up, literally. We need to operate on the same level of faith. Whatever God says is wrong is wrong. We should not bend His Word to fit our situation. It is wrong to lie and gossip. It is wrong to spread discord with rumors and cause problems for others. It is wrong to think evil thoughts about someone who has wronged us.

In conclusion, it should be evident in the way we live and talk that we are Christians. Let your light shine. Be bold in the things of God even when the heat is intensified.

Comfort Zones

Day 15
Prayer: Dear Heavenly Father, I am so grateful that You know what's best for me. Thank you for stretching, molding, and purging me. You are in charge of my life. I will let you lead. In Jesus's name I pray, amen.

Scripture: Now the Lord had said to Abram: "Get out of your country, From your family And from your father's house, To a land that I will show you. Genesis 12:1 NKJV

We are very familiar with comfort zones. How many of us motivate our students or children to move from their comfort zones to try something new? We encourage them to explore their gifts, talents, and stretch their minds. That's wonderful, but what about us. Are we willing to get out of our comfort zones? I am guilty of becoming complacent. We cannot grow and excel when we're complacent. It is ok to stretch and leave your comfort zone.

My student-teaching was completed in a first grade classroom. Then I taught first grade for nine years. One day, the principal told me I was moving to fifth grade. I instantly became nervous and anxious. My faith went out the window. I thought, first grade is all I know. Fifth graders are older and mean. Why me? Oh my, I have to brush up on all that new material! So much went through my mind. Instead, I should have been thinking "I can do all things through Christ who strengthens me." (Philippians 4:13 NKJV)

Little did I know, God was stretching and preparing me for something greater. I absolutely loved teaching fifth grade! I cried like a baby when I had to leave my fifth graders (who were not mean, as I originally thought) to go teach fourth grade. I fell in love with teaching fourth grade as well. I really was stretched out of my comfort zone when I taught sixth grade for summer school, but I enjoyed every minute of it.

Abram was definitely stretched out of his comfort zone. God instructed him to leave family and travel until He said stop. God pulls us out of our comfort zones to see if we really trust Him. Abram trusted God, and became the father of many nations (Genesis 17:4) and the father of faith. Do you trust God? Will you go when he says go? Will you have that tough conversation with a parent, coworker, principal, family member, or student?

In conclusion, the only way to grow and have a deeper relationship with God is to get out of our comfort zones. We have to do something we don't usually do. Do not worry. If God is directing you out of your comfort zone, He's not going to leave you.

A Man on A Mission

Day 16

Prayer: Dear Heavenly Father, You are such a faithful God. I'm grateful for every promise in your Word. It is Your promises that give me strength to keep pushing forward. Thank you for always keeping your word. You are my all and I can't do anything without You. Help me to keep leaning on You. In Jesus's name I pray, amen.

Scripture: The Lord is not slack concerning His promise, as some count slackness, but is long suffering toward us, not willing that any should perish but that all should come to repentance. 2 Peter 3:9 NKJV

Have you been waiting for a really long time for God to move on your behalf? Have you been trusting Him for a breakthrough in a particular area of your life? Whatever God has promised you, He'll give it to you. He promised Abraham that he would be the father of many nations. There were many years between God's promise and Isaac's birth, but God did not lie.

How would you react if God's promise finally manifested in your life? Of course, you would be grateful and singing praises.

What if God tells you to sacrifice what you have been waiting on for so long? That is what happened to Abraham when God instructed him to sacrifice Issac, but he stood firmly on God's promise. Abraham held tightly to the promise that he'd be the father of many nations as he climbed the mountain to sacrifice Issac. Abraham knew that God would work it out, otherwise how could his descendants number the stars and grains of sand (Genesis 22:17).

In conclusion, what has God asked you to sacrifice? Will you hold on to it rather than be obedient? Trust Him to have your ram in the bush (Genesis 22:13). Or will you be like Abraham, who was on a mission to follow God's instructions? Abraham was so focused on being obedient that the angel had to call his name twice (Genesis 22:11). Will you have that focus in your classroom? Do you believe that God will be faithful? Trust Him with everything in every situation.

The Powerful Strategist

DAY 17

Prayer:
Lord, You are the author and finisher of my faith. I trust You and Your plan for my life. I bind the enemy's plan for my life. I decree and declare that I will walk in the destiny that You've designed for me. Thank you for delivering me from the snare of the fowler. I'm grateful for Your manifested protection over my life. Take over me. Holy Spirit have your way in my life. In Jesus's name I pray, amen.

Scripture: For I know the thoughts that I think toward you, says the Lord , thoughts of peace and not of evil, to give you a future and a hope.
Jeremiah 29:11 NKJV

Teachers are familiar with writing various styles of lesson plans for different subject
areas. Have you given any thought as to how the lesson plans impact your students' future? Have

you thought about their futures pass the period or block that they are in your class? I encourage you to look at the bigger picture. It is not just a lesson on a particular skill.

For example, when you are teaching place value, that's a lifelong skill that students can use to be good stewards over their finances. When you're teaching a language lesson, you're giving your students skills to be effective speakers and writers, like Paul, who wrote nearly all the New Testament. God has a plan for each of our lives. He gives us strategies to be successful.

For example, during a battle God instructed Joshua to burn his enemy's chariots and cripple their horses (Joshua 11:6). That was a successful strategy to win.

You aren't insignificant in your students' future. You play a vital part in molding and shaping their minds and futures. What you do in your classroom is extremely important. Do not ever downplay your role in their lives.

By Any Means Necessary

DAY 18

Prayer: Heavenly Father, I seek You for all my help in my classroom. I know that there isn't anything impossible for You. I will go over and beyond to experience your glory. Pour into me Lord. In Jesus's name I pray, amen.

Scripture: So he ran ahead and climbed up into a sycamore tree to see Him, for He was going to pass that way. Luke 19:4 NKJV

Students like to get their teacher's approval. They feel like they have accomplished something or finally reached a goal when their teacher praises them. Some students will go the extra mile and push a little harder to win the teacher's approval. What are you doing to get God's approval? Are you going the extra mile in your prayer life? Are you pressing into God harder during worship?

Of course the enemy doesn't want you to be successful in your career. Nor does he want your students to progress. Satan is ruthless and will do anything to keep you, as well as your students, burnt out, depressed, sluggish, and complacent. So, you have to be strong, bold, and forceful in your prayer life and worship. The woman who had the issue of blood for 12 years

pushed through a crowd just to touch Jesus's clothes (Mark 5:27-28). She refused to lie down in

defeat. She was not going to give the devil a victory. She got to Jesus by any means necessary.

Similarly, Zacchaeus wanted to see Jesus so badly that he climbed a tree (Luke 19:4). Likewise,

Hannah went the extra mile praying hard from her heart for a child. She prayed so passionately

and fervently that the prophet thought she was drunk (1 Samuel 1:13).

In conclusion, to have victory in life as well as your classroom, press harder into the

Lord. Dig deeper into the things of God. Worship like no one is watching, David did (2 Samuel

6:14-22)!

Peace Keeper

Day 19

Prayer: Heavenly Father, thank you for giving me peace. I'm grateful that You are in control of my life. Guard my tongue so I only use it to please you. In Jesus' name I pray, amen.

Scripture: Blessed are the peacemakers, For they shall be called sons of God. Matthew 5:9 NKJV

We all want to live in peace. We want peace at work, at home, and in our relationships. How do we obtain and maintain peace?

Simply invite Jesus into your workplace, home, and relationships. Jesus is the Prince of Peace (Isaiah 9:6 NKJV). Jesus instructs us to pursue peace with everyone (Hebrews 12:14). As you are conferencing with a difficult parent or student, invite Jesus into the conversation. He'll grace

your words. He'll shift the atmosphere. Let Him.

Which Way?

DAY 20 Prayer: My Lord and Savior, thank you for showing me the route to take. Thank you for paving the way. I will continue to lean on You for guidance. Amen.

Scripture: Jesus said to him, "I am the way, the truth, and the life. No one comes to the Father except through Me. John 14:6 NKJV

Where are you going? More importantly, who is leading you there? Each morning that you rise ask Jesus to go before you. Ask Him to direct your path in every area. It is not trivial or paranoia to ask Him to lead everything. When you are on your way to work, ask Him which route is best. The enemy may have a trap waiting on you on a certain road. If you use public transportation, ask Jesus where to sit. There may be someone who needs to hear a word from you. Ask Jesus where to park when you're going to the supermarket. 1 Thessalonians 5:17 instructs us to pray without cease. I remember when I was shopping for the dress I wanted to wear for my wedding reception.

I kept trying on dress after dress and praying. I am so thankful that I was in the store so long, because I didn't know there was someone robbing people in the parking lot! By the time I was checking out, police had arrived.

I have been in situations when the Holy Spirit would lead me to take a different route to work. I would find out later that a horrible accident occurred on my usual route. Jesus is full of infinite wisdom. Let's let the wisest help us choose which way.

FAITHFULNESS

DAY 21

Prayer: Lord, you are always faithful. There is no one as faithful as You. I'm grateful for that. Help me to be more like you. In Jesus' name I pray, amen.

Scripture: "God is not a man, that He should lie, Nor a son of man, that He should repent. Has He said, and will He not do? Or has He spoken, and will He not make it good? Numbers 23:19 NKJV

I am sure we've all expected someone to do something that they said they would. Or we have given someone our word that we'll be somewhere or do something. Well, sometimes it does not happen that way. We are human. We may have forgotten, gotten too busy, or finally really thought about it and simply did not want to do it anymore. I am guilty of all the above. I have a habit of getting excited and agreeing to do something before checking it out thoroughly.

It amazes me how faithful God is to us. We will give our word and not follow through. God gives His word and always follows through. His word is a promise. So, whatever He has spoken to you or shown you, it's a promise. The most beautiful part is that He cannot lie. Hold on to every promise or vision He's given you for your career, family, marriage, etc. He's faithful.

The Long Way Home

DAY 22 Prayer: Father, thank you for being there for me. Thank you for watching over me. Help me to make wise decisions. In Jesus' name I pray, amen.

Scripture:"And he arose and came to his father. But when he was still a great way off, his father saw him and had compassion, and ran and fell on his neck and kissed him. Luke 15:20 NKJV

Jesus loves you and intercedes for you (Hebrews 7:25). If you have gotten off track in your prayer life and in your spiritual walk, it's not too late to make a change. The prodigal son made a rash and poor decision to leave home and squander all he had. If you have made a poor choice, it's not too late to make it right. Go to them and apologize. That is what the prodigal son did. It may not be easy, but it is humbling. Humble people are teachable people. God would rather you be humble (Proverbs 16:19 & Matthew 23:12). A prideful heart leads to destruction

(Proverbs 16:18). I encourage you to right any wrongs that you are aware of. Live in peace.

Busy Bee

DAY 23 Prayer: Heavenly Father, please forgive me if I lose sight of the bigger picture of giving You glory at all times. Please don't allow me to be so busy with work that I forget who I am working for. In Jesus' name I pray, amen.

Scripture: And Jesus answered and said to her, "Martha, Martha, you are worried and troubled about many things. But one thing is needed, and Mary has chosen that good part, which will not be taken away from her." Luke 10:41-42 NKJV

We are always moving. We are always running about to do an errand of some kind. Rush. Rush. Rush. Luke 10 speaks of how busy Martha was serving and making sure the house was presentable. She was so busy working that she lost sight of who she was working for. Jesus was literally in her living room and she was missing what He had to say! Could you imagine Jesus visiting your home and you are so busy picking up toys, washing the pile of laundry, and washing dishes that you ignore Him? That is so sad, but it happens. We get so caught up in the business of life that we forget the creator of life.

I encourage you to be more like Mary, Martha's sister, and sit at Jesus's feet. Take in everything He has to offer. Welcome Him into your heart and life.

No, no Naaman

Day 24 Dear merciful Father, I repent. Please forgive me for wanting a breakthrough my way. I can not tell you how or when to move. My job is to believe that You can and will according to Your Word. In Jesus's name, I pray amen.

Scripture: Isaiah 55:8-9 "For My thoughts are not your thoughts, Nor are your ways My ways", says the Lord. "For as the heaven are higher than the earth, So are My ways higher than your ways. And My thoughts than your thoughts.

We have all been in need of breakthroughs at one time or another. There have been times when I have wanted to speed up the process leading up to my breakthrough. I have learned that I cannot rush the process. It is not physically possible (nor would I dare if it was) march to Heaven and request that God get to moving. He has promises throughout His Word that He has a plan for us (Jeremiah 29:11). He wants us to have good success and be prosperous according to Joshua 1:8.

Naaman was a commander in the army and held great honor (2 Kings 5). Naaman was mighty, but he had leprosy. His wife's servant was from Israel and knew how God was using the prophet Elisha to heal. The servant mentioned this to Naaman's wife, who mentioned it to Naaman. So of course, Naaman was eager to go see Elisha. When Naaman got to Elisha's house, a messenger was sent out to him according to 2 Kings 5:9-10. Elisha knew Naaman was coming to his house, because he was the one who told the king to send Naaman there (2 Kings 5:8). Here is when Naaman messes up and acts ugly. He got mad because Elisha did not come out, wave his hands over the leprosy, and pray. Instead, Elisha simply instructed his messenger to give Naaman a set of directions. Naaman was to wash in the Jordan River seven times and be cleansed. Well, Naaman did not want to hear that. He thought his healing was supposed to happen another way. He thought he could tell God how to heal him. Nevertheless, Naaman was not crazy. He sucked it up, quit fussing, and went to the Jordan River to wash and be healed. Afterwards, he was glad he did follow the prophet's directions. It is important to trust God. Trust His process. He knows what is best for us because He created us.

ZIP IT!

Day 25 Prayer: Gracious Heavenly Father, thank you for teaching me when to speak and when to keep quiet. Help me to be sensitive to your Holy Spirit. Guide me on who to share and not share information with as you give me revelation and knowledge.

Scripture: Genesis 37:5 NKJV Now Joseph had a dream, and he told it to his brothers; and they hated him even more.

Joseph was a dreamer. God would speak to Joseph through prophetic dreams. Joseph was already hated by his older brothers because their father favored him. After he shared his dream with his brothers, they hated him much more (Genesis 37: 7-8). The dream depicted Joseph's brothers bowing to him. The idea of them bowing to their younger brother infuriated them.

Apparently, Joseph did not learn his lesson the first time he overshared. God gave him a second prophetic dream about his family bowing to him. This time he shared it with his brothers and father. Later in the text, Joseph's brothers plot his demise and sell him (Genesis 37: 21-28).

Sometimes, we get so excited when God reveals His plans to us. It is hard to not share. I warn you that not everyone will be genuinely happy for you when God sees fit to promote you.

Do not be surprised if your family members or phony friends are not running to support you. The spirit of jealousy does not care about how you are related to a person. It was Joseph's own brothers who thought of murdering him. Jealousy is a wicked and dangerous spirit. It is destructive to operate in jealousy. If you know that someone is jealous of you, I advise you to keep your plans, dreams, and goals to yourself, because the spirit of jealousy will begin to plot your demise. "Wrath is cruel and anger a torrent, But who is able to stand before jealousy?" Proverbs 27:4 NKJV

WRESTLING

Day 26

Prayer: Lord, You are so great and mighty. There is no one more wonderful than You. You are the God who provides for us, Jehovah-Jireh. Thank you for blessing me beyond what I can ever imagine. In Jesus' name I pray, amen.

Scripture: Genesis 32: 26 NKJV And He said, "Let Me go, for the day breaks." But he said, "I will not let You go unless You bless me!"

We all want God's promises to manifest in our lives. We want to live out the blessings listed in Deuteronomy 28: 1-14. What is stopping you? There may be different reasons, but you must fight. It will not be easy, but the Word instructs us to fight (1 Timothy 6:12 and 2 Timothy 4: 7). Jacob put up a good fight by refusing to give up even though he was severely hurt. His hip bone was out of socket from this wrestling match, but he kept going.

Are you willing to keep fighting the good fight of faith when the situation seems unbearable? When you are in pain? When you are tired? When you feel like you just cannot go another hour under so much stress? Jacob could and did. Jacob absolutely refused to stop fighting. He wrestled all night long for his blessing. How far and how long are you willing to go? Proverbs 24:10 NKJV states, "if you faint in the day of adversity than your strength is small." This means that if you buckle or crack under pressure, your faith was not worth much. You cannot grumble and complain while your fighting for you blessing. Jacob did not complain even when his hip was out of socket. Jacob did not care how many hours had passed. The sun was about to rise, and Jacob was prepared to keep fighting another day if required. I encourage you to not give up. Fight. Fight some more. Do not let go until you see the manifestation of your breakthrough.

FASTING

Day 27

Prayer: Father, I find strength in you. I need Your help with crucifying my flesh and strengthening my spirit. Please give me grace to push my plate back and have self-control. I repent for letting my stomach be my god. You are the one true and living God who gives me joy. In Jesus's name I pray, amen.

Scripture: Mark 9:29 NKJV So He said to them,"This kind can come out by nothing but prayer and fasting."

Is living a life of fasting impossible? Why does the Bible instruct us to crucify our flesh daily? It is not impossible to live a life of fasting. If it were, Jesus would not have demonstrated how it could be done. He fasted for 40 days. So, for 40 days, Jesus crucified His flesh and fed His Spirit. The devil loves when we starve or neglect our spirit and feed our flesh. We feed our flesh by giving into our own desires. You should not give your flesh everything it wants. The more you feed your flesh, the more you weaken your spirit. If your spirit is weak, how can you stand and fight spiritual battles? In Ephesians 6, we are told to stand multiple times. Your spirit will not be able to stand or withstand if it has been starved and deprived. Now, you are probably wondering how do you feed your spirit? Jesus gave the perfect response when the devil was tempting Him after His fast ended. But He answered and said, "It is written,'Man shall not live by bread alone, but by every word that proceeds from the mouth of God.'" Matthew 4:4 NKJV So, you feed your spirit by reading the Word of God. You may be thinking, how could reading the Word make my spirit strong to be able to stand against the wiles of the devil (Ephesians 6:10- 11)? Well, part of the armor of the Lord is the sword of the Spirit. Notice this time the word spirit is written with the letter 's' in uppercase. This signifies that the scripture is referring to God's Spirit. Part of the armor used to destroy attacks of the enemy during spiritual battles is the Word. How does the Word abort the devil's missions? Hebrews 4:12 NKJV gives a great explanation.

The Word is so powerful because it is God according to John 1:1 "In the beginning was the Word, and the Word was with God, and the Word was God". It is impossible for the devil to stand against the Word. He is NOT more powerful than God. This is why the devil does not want you to feed your spirit. When you know the Word and speak it, it is a mighty weapon to crush the attacks of the enemy and his demons. Why would the devil want you to use a weapon against him? Satan will use every tactic he has to discourage you from fasting. There is no way that the enemy can defeat a fasting and praying Christian. Therefore it is vital to fast. I encourage you to strengthen your spirit for the battle. For the word of God is living and powerful, and sharper than any two-edged sword, piercing even to the division of soul and spirit, and of joints and marrow, and is a discerner of the thoughts and intents of the heart. Hebrews 4:12 NKJV

Have You Had Enough Yet?

Day 28 Prayer: Father, I ask that you forgive me for the times when I thought Your Word was not enough. I repent for making you angry by constantly asking for a sign. I repent for not believing in You as I should. I am sorry. I ask that You help me to have confidence in You. Help me to read Your Word and literally believe all of it. Thank you for being patient with me as I grow in the knowledge of Your kingdom. In Jesus's name I pray, amen.

Scripture: 1 Corinthians 15:57 NKJV But thanks be to God, who gives us the victory through our Lord Jesus Christ.

It is so comforting and reassuring to know that whatever God says is enough. His Word is the final say in any situation. I love 1 Corinthians 15:57. This scripture means we win! Defeat is not an option for a believer. God does not fail, so it is impossible to fail with Christ as your Lord.

This concept of victory and God's Word being the

final say was a little hard for Gideon to understand. Judges 6 opens by explaining the horror and hardship the children of Israel were going through at the time. I suggest that you take some time and read the whole chapter to see why life was so hard for them. To make a long story short, the children of Israel were living in fear inside of caves and dens in the mountains. It was a life of constant torment and oppression for seven years. Year after year, the Midianites, Amalekites and the people of the East would destroy the children of Israel's crops and livestock (Judges 6:5). There were so many enemies coming against them at one time that they could not count them.

Had the children of Israel had enough yet? Have you been in a similar situation? Have you ever felt like you were being hit by the enemy in every area of your life? The children of Israel had finally had enough, so they turned back to God for help (they should have never turned away from Him). After God sent a prophet to remind them of how they disobeyed Him, He helped. He chose to use Gideon from the tribe of Mannaseh to lead the battle against their enemies. There was one issue with this. Gideon had a hard time believing the Lord when He said they would have victory (Judges 6:15-17). Please do not make this same mistake and anger God. When the Lord offers a strategy for you to come out of debt, sickness, oppression, or whatever, it is best to listen and obey. His strategies may seem odd or illogical, but they work every time. That is why His thoughts are higher than ours

(Isaiah 55:8-9). Poor Gideon asked God for a few signs before he finally believed Him. God can not lie (Numbers 23:19).

Unlike Gideon, a widow was in debt and needed an immediate breakthrough, but she did not question the Lord's strategy (2 Kings 4). The widow was overwhelmed with her deceased husband's debt and faced with losing her sons because of it. When the prophet Elisha told her to go borrow empty jars from neighbors, she did not lose her temper or become doubtful. I can imagine that if she had not had faith that she would have said, "Elisha, did you not hear me? I need money now! They are coming to take my sons as slaves!" Instead she went right on and followed his instructions, which were from the Lord (2 Kings 4:5). The debt was cancelled immediately because she was obedient. Has God ever given you a strategy , but you thought it was so absurd that you dismissed the thought? If you have had enough, do not dismiss the Lord's strategies.

FEAR

Day 29

Prayer: Most gracious Father, I am thankful for the mercy You have shown me. Thank you for new mercies each day. I repent for operating in fear. Please forgive me for my lack of faith. I pray that my faith strengthens and is rooted in the Rock of Ages. I release Your all-consuming fire on every seed of doubt that the enemy has planted in my mind. Let those seeds burn to the root and be removed from my mind. I pray that every righteous seed that has been planted in me, take deep root and flourish like foliage. I want to please you in every way, in Jesus's name, I pray amen.

Scripture: Hebrews 11: 6 NKJV But without faith it is impossible to please Him, for he who comes to God must believe that He is, and that He is a rewarder of those who diligently seek Him.

Fear is a spirit from darkness and is given by the devil. Are you wondering why I called fear a spirit? How do I know that fear is not given to us by God? The answers to these questions are in the Word.

According to Psalms 27:1, God is our light and salvation. Where there is light, darkness flees. Light and darkness cannot be in the same location. When you are fully suited in the armor of

God (Ephesians 6:13), you are wearing the helmet of salvation. In the natural, a helmet is a tool of protection to safeguard the brain, which is needed for us to function. The armor of God is For God has not given us a spirit of fear, but of power and of love and of a sound mind. 2 Timothy 1:7 NKJV spiritual, which means it is invisible; therefore, the helmet of salvation protects our mind as a natural helmet would protect our brain.

When the devil gives fear, he plants it as thoughts in your mind. That is why the helmet of salvation is a vital piece of armor. It is a weapon to protect your mind! Jesus offers salvation. Salvation is not only fire insurance to save you from going to hell, but it's a current protection as a helmet from the tormenting spirit of fear. This tormenting spirit is described in 1 John 4:18. I suggest that you pray on the armor of God daily and declare that you have a mind like Christ as it is written in 1st Corinthians 2:16. Gird the loins of your mind as we are advised to in 1 Peter 1:13. gird means to fasting or prepare. During the time this was written long roads were worn.

Before a battle, the long robes would be girded, which meant securing or tucking the robe into their belt to avoid tripping. When you gird the lawns of your mind, you control your thoughts. By controlling your thoughts, you do not trip and fall into fear or allow other sins to control your mind. Fight the negative thoughts which are really snares from the enemy with 2 Corinthians 10:3-5. Make all your thoughts obey Christ.

Just Let Me Get There

Day 30 Prayer: Lord, You are so great and powerful. There is no one greater than you. I love you and love being in your presence. I am grateful that you will never leave me. I cannot make it without your spirit, your glory, your mercy, and your grace. Thank you Lord!

Scripture: Isaiah 25:1 NKJV O Lord, You are my God. I will exalt You, I will praise Your name, For You have done wonderful things; Your counsels of old are faithfulness and truth.

I have had some days when I would say, " If I could just get in my prayer closet; if I can just make it to prayer service." Do not get me wrong. I know God is omnipresent, everywhere at the same time. There is just something about a designated meeting place with the Lord that is powerful. There is something unique that happens when we are in His presence. When I am in His presence, it is incredible and indescribable. I wish I could put into words how I feel when I ask to be invaded and engulfed with His Holy Spirit. Nothing else matters when I am focused on getting into his presence and communicating with Him. God's presence shifts the atmosphere. The best way I can get you to really understand this is to explain my need to be in God's presence as a craving. It is like I cannot breathe without His Word. Luke expounds on a similar feeling in Acts 17: 28. We cannot do anything without Jesus. We need him when things are going well and when we are going through a rough time. I feel like the church is described as a bride and Christ described as a bridegroom in the scriptures is because a bride and a bridegroom have a relationship in the marriage. And our Lord wants to have a relationship with us. If you are a dating someone now there are times when you just cannot wait to see them. You cannot wait to talk to them on the phone. You are looking for the next text from them. You just love to be near them. You are in love with them. If you are already married you just cannot wait until your spouse gets home from work. You love when you all spend time together. You look for those special text messages. You look for those sweet phone calls. It is just an amazing feeling to be in a good healthy relationship with someone whom you love and the feeling is mutual. That is how I feel about Christ. I love him so much that I just cannot wait to get close to him. I cannot wait to be in his presence. It is so comforting and it feels so good. He knows me very well and I am getting to know him better as each day passes.

How is your relationship with Christ? Do you only

call him when you need something? Do you look forward to when he calls on you to do something? Are you excited to spend time with him in prayer and worship? Take a second and think about that. The relationship is only as good as the communication that you have with one another. If you only talk once a week, that is not much of a relationship. If you only spend time together two Sundays out of the month that is not a very good relationship. Jesus wants to spend time with you every day. He loves you. He should be your first love. Christ longs for a deep, solid relationship with us. He is standing at the door of our hearts knocking. When someone is knocking, that person seeks your permission to answer. Having a relationship with Jesus means knowing his voice. Jesus explains this relationship in John 10: 3-5. If you spend time with someone on a daily basis, you undoubtedly know their voice. Are you ready for a deeper connection with the Holy Spirit? Are you willing to sacrifice something so he can move freely in your life? About three years ago I began making lifestyle changes so developing a relationship with the Holy Spirit became a priority. I begin setting my alarm for 5 a.m. 3 days a week to call my church's prayer line. We pray from 5 a.m. until 6 a.m. every Monday, Wednesday, and Friday. I also exchanged three of my favorite TV shows for studying the Word and reading books about spiritual warfare and deliverance. These TV shows are an hour long. So that was three additional hours given to the Lord. My drive to work is 45 minutes one way. I stopped listening to secular music during my drive. Instead I used that time to worship. That is an additional 90 minutes (both ways). I did not tell you all that to get any reward. I just wanted to share practical ways to get closer to Jesus. You must give up some worldly habits, but what we gain far outweighs any TV show or amount of sleep.

Go deeper one day at a time. Be blessed.

NOTES:

believe

So they said, "Believe on the Lord Jesus Christ, and you will be saved, you and your household."
Acts 16:31 NKJV

Because it is written, "Be holy, for I am holy."
1 Peter 1:16 NKJV

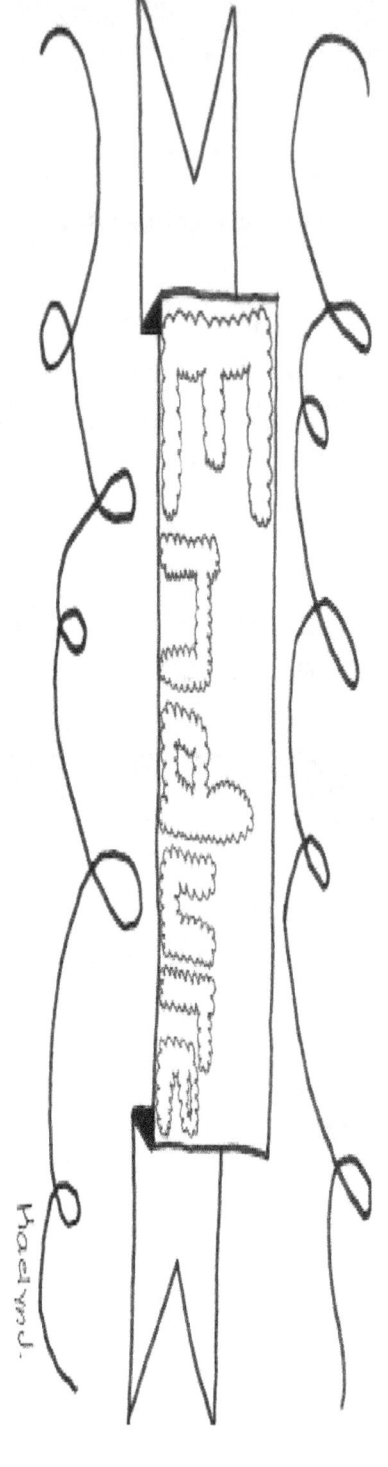

You therefore must endure hardship as a good soldier of Jesus Christ
2 Timothy 2:3
NKJV

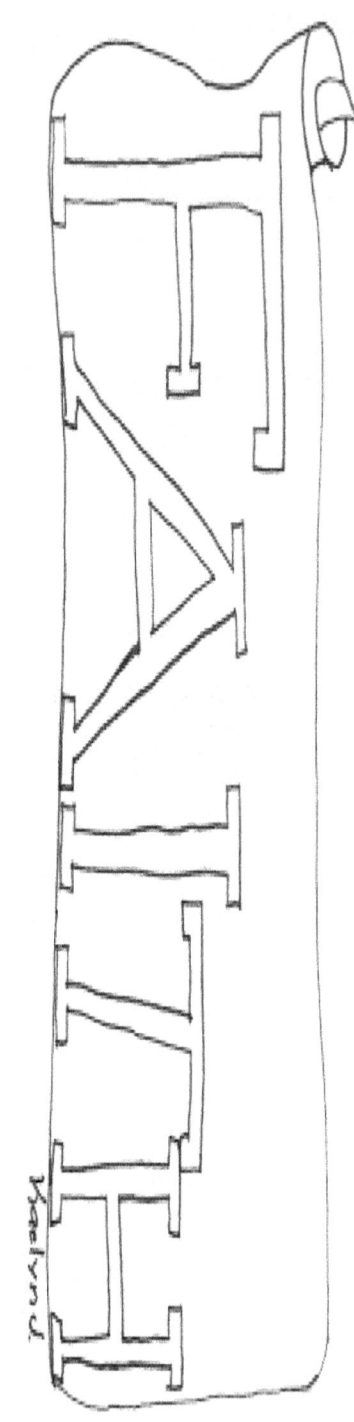

But without faith it is impossible to please Him

Hebrews 11:6

NKJV

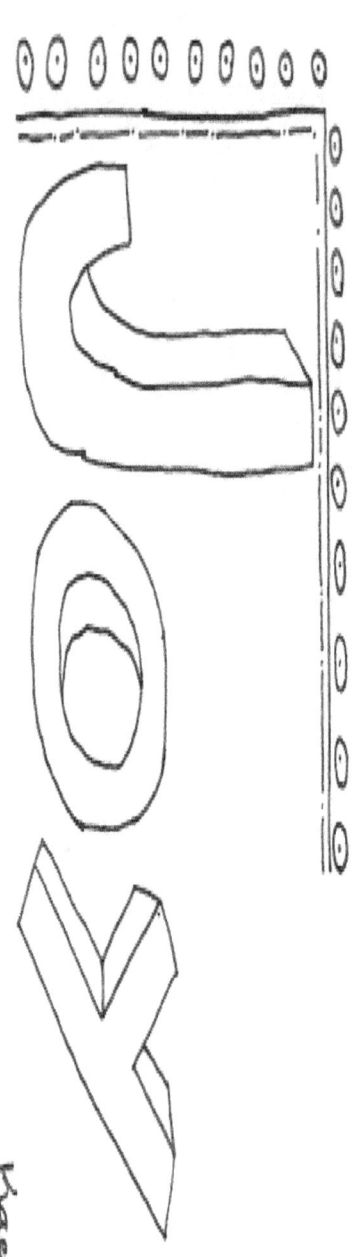

Do not sorrow, for the joy of the Lord is your strength.
Nehemiah 8:10 NKJV

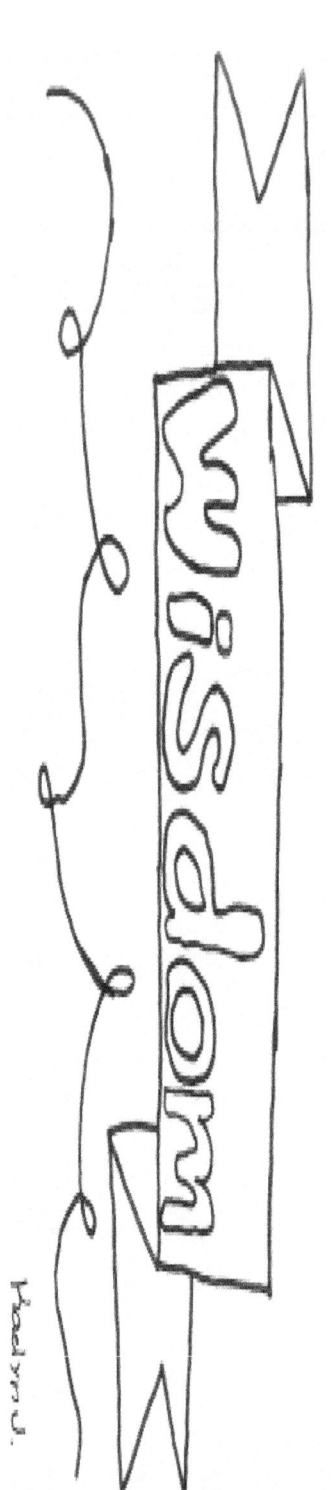

Wisdom is the principal thing; Therefore get wisdom. And in all your getting, get understanding.
Proverbs 4:7 NKJV

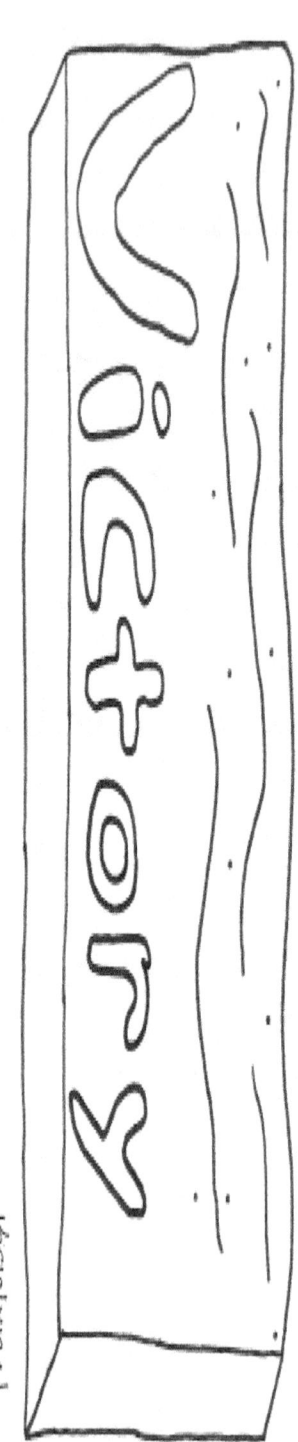

BUT THANKS BE TO GOD, WHO GIVES US THE VICTORY THROUGH OUR LORD JESUS CHRIST.
1 CORINTHIANS 15:57 NKJV

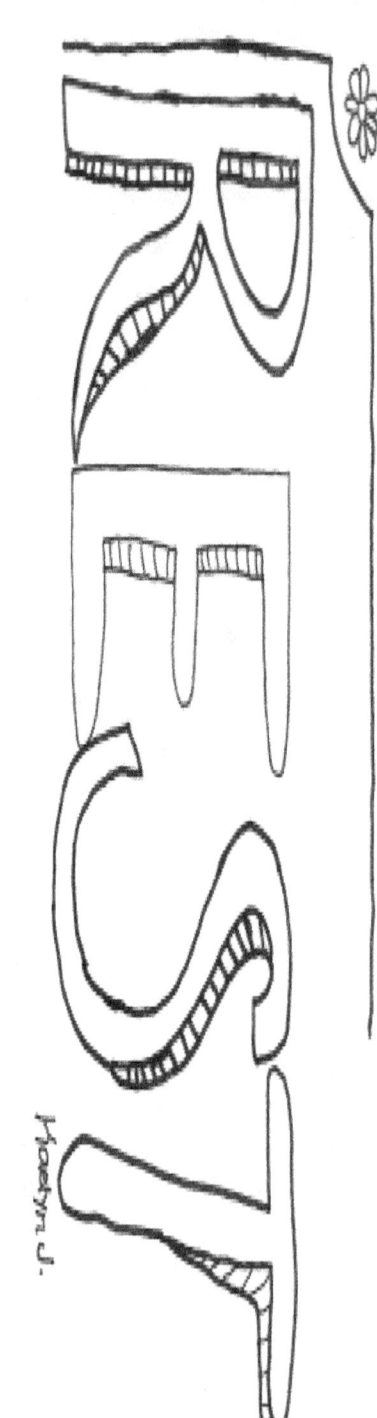

Rest in the LORD, and wait patiently for Him
Psalm 37:7
NKJV

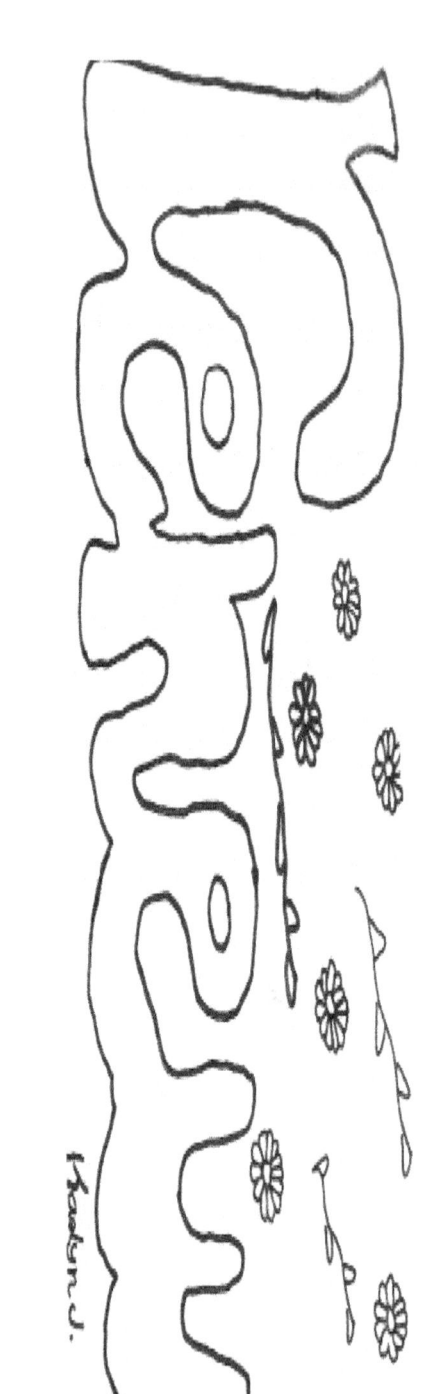

But those who wait on the LORD shall renew their strength

Isaiah 40:31

NKJV

and the peace of God, which surpasses all understanding, will guard your hearts and minds through Christ Jesus.
Philippians 4:7
NKJV

Author's Note

Thank you for the support. I hope that this book is a blessing to your life. Most of the experiences in this devotional occurred while I was teaching in a school district. You can read about my phases of life and transition in my previous book, Doing All God Has Called You To Do: A Devotion for Novice Teachers. There are several entries that are written from a teacher's point of view, but God's law is always applicable to all situations. The Lord has blessed me to walk a different path with education. We are all teachers in some fashion.

Be Blessed

www.ingramcontent.com/pod-product-compliance
Lightning Source LLC
Chambersburg PA
CBHW052115110526
44592CB00013B/1626